SIMPLIFY AND CREATE ABUNDANCE

How to Be Really Wealthy
Without Robbing Your Soul

BO SANCHEZ

Best-selling author of *Simplify and Live the Good Life*
and *You Have the Power to Create Love*

SHEPHERD'S
V O I C E

OTHER BOOKS BY BO SANCHEZ

THE BOSS Series
Thank God He's Boss
You Can Make Your Life Beautiful
You Have the Power to Create Love

SIMPLIFY Series
Simplify and Live the Good Life
Simplify and Create Abundance

PRAYERBOOKS
Embraced
The Way of the Cross
Special Prayers for the Rosary

SIMPLIFY AND CREATE ABUNDANCE
How to Be Really Wealthy Without Robbing Your Soul

Love God!

SIMPLIFY AND CREATE ABUNDANCE
How to Be Really Wealthy Without Robbing Your Soul

ISBN- 971-92613-1-5

BO SANCHEZ
Best-selling author of *Simplify and Live the Good Life*
and *You Have the Power to Create Love*

Requests for information should be addressed to:
SHEPHERD'S VOICE PUBLICATIONS, INC.
#60 Chicago St., Cubao, Quezon City, Philippines 1109
Tel. No. (02) 411-7874 to77
e-mail: sale@shepherdsvoice.com.ph

Layout design by Rey de Guzman

CONTENTS

Many of life's failures are people who did not realize
how close they were to success when they gave up.
—Thomas Edison

INTRODUCTION

NEVER FORGET THIS IS A JOURNEY

Remember how the Lord your God led you on this long
journey through the desert these past forty years…
He made you go hungry, and then he gave you
manna to eat…. The Lord your God is bringing you
into a fertile land—there you will never
go hungry or ever be in need.
—Deuteronomy 8:2-10

Everywhere I go, I share my crazy doughnut experience.

So much so that people have called me the doughnut man.

My hope is that this doesn't reflect a numerical value.

This is what happened.

When I was 16 years old, a friend and I were walking in a commercial center.

As we walked, I felt my tummy grumble.

I turned to my companion and asked, "Are you hungry?"

She nodded.

I searched for cash in my pockets and found none. That was no surprise. Actually, if I had found money, I would have wondered if I had worn someone else's pants.

I asked my friend again, "Do you have money?"

"Nope," she said, "I thought you had money."

Her answer revealed how much she didn't know me. In the meantime, my hunger pangs became more acute as I sensed the aroma of doughnuts wafting through the air. (I have the unique ability to smell doughnuts a mile away.)

I looked up at the sky and semi-complained, "Lord, what are you going to do about our hunger?"

That was when a crazy idea hit my head.

I told my friend, "Hey, let's just go into this doughnut shop and *smell!*"

"Just *smell?* That's all we'll do?"

"Yes!" I said. "And let's have faith that God will fill up our stomachs!"

So we marched in, looked at the colorful doughnuts in front of us, and prayed, "Bless us, oh Lord, and the food which we are to receive…"

Then we started smelling with gusto. Mmmmm!

That was when I heard a guy call my name from the back of the eatery.

"Bo!" the distinguished looking man hollered, waving at me.

I waved back at him and smiled my friendliest smile. I also whispered to my friend, "Do you know who this guy is waving at me?"

"Don't have a clue," she said.

He walked up to me and said, "Hi, Bo!"

I answered, "Hi! Long time no see!"

After a few more hi's, I asked, "By the way, what's your name?"

"My name is John!" he laughed.

The conversation became better after that until he asked me a question that was incredibly difficult to answer: "Bo, what are you doing here?"

I just knew that "smelling" was not going to be a good answer at all.

A light bulb turned on my head. "Uhh… we were just taking a breather," I said. I had to change the topic right away so I asked, "John, what are you doing here?"

"Me? I'm the manager of this doughnut shop."

My chinky eyes became large as saucers.

"Oh… you're the manager…"

Already, I could hear Handel's *Hallelujah Chorus* being played in the background.

"Yes. Why don't you and your friend line up and get as many doughnuts as you want. They're on the house."

That day, I ate 31 doughnuts.

GOD IS A GOD OF MIRACLES

My friends, that's manna.

A miraculous blessing from God at the time you need it most.

I can fill this entire book with manna stories from my life.

When the Israelites were hungry, God sent them bread each morning. When they woke up, manna was found on the desert sands.

I believe that to this day, when we travel our desert of financial difficulty, God still gives us manna. He gives us miracles every day!

How many times I've heard stories like this one I cannot count: Enrollment season is coming and the mother has no idea where to get money for her kid's tuition. But on the day before the deadline, a letter arrives from an aunt in the US (or Australia, or Canada, or Italy…) and though this person hasn't written for three centuries, in the envelope is a check. And it's always the exact amount needed.

Inspiring, isn't it? But here's our problem: Some people think that receiving manna in the desert is God's desired destination for us. Let me shock you. It *isn't* our destination.

He wants you to enter the Promised Land.[1]

He wants you to enter a place which I call Simple Abundance.

That's where He wants you to go.

He doesn't just want you to wait for manna to fall from the sky. He actually wants you to enter the Promised Land, where you'll till the soil, plant the seed and harvest the crops! And yes, receive even more abundant miracles from Him!

This is my message in this book: From a state of not having enough (the desert), you move to a state of having enough (the desert with manna). But ultimately, God wants you to move to a state where you have more than enough—the Promised Land, or the place of Simple Abundance.

I believe He wants you to move into Simple Abundance where you can share your blessings with others.

Don't get stuck in the desert.

And as wonderful as manna is, don't get stuck with it either.

Here's what I mean.

GO TO THE PROMISED LAND

A friend of mine drives this special car.

He says it doesn't run on diesel or gasoline—it runs on faith. Because there are days when the car's fuel tank is empty and he has no money to buy gasoline. So he prays over the car and it works for a few more days until he has money to buy gas.

And there are mornings when he can't start his car. So he lays his hand on the dashboard and prays over the car. After a few failed attempts at the ignition, and a few more desperate praying-in-tongues and refrains of the song "Come Holy Spirit, I Need You," the engine purrs and comes alive.

My friend says, "Bo, this has been going on for a year now. This is a miracle car!" And he asks me, "Do these miracles happen to you as well?"

I smile, "Yes, but my miracles are a bit different now."

"What do you mean?"

"I never run out of gas because I fill up the gas tank every time I need to. I also buy a new car battery every 18 months. That's why my car starts every morning."

He frowns, "What's so exciting about that? Where's the miracle?"

"The miracle," I announce, "is that I can now afford to buy a full tank of fuel and a new battery every 18 months! The miracle is that God is using my itsy-bitsy teeny-weeny businesses to provide for my needs!"

You see, the manna experience was designed by God to teach us an *attitude*, not a behavior.

I told my friend to start moving to the Promised Land.

My dear reader, I ask you to do the same.

Move to the place of Simple Abundance because God wants to use you to provide for the needs of the Church and the poor.

How do you do that?

Read on.

GET THE DESERT OUT OF YOU

Are you going through financial difficulties?

Where you are now need not be a permanent situation.

This isn't your life.

This isn't the destination.

This is just a stopover—a very important stopover with lessons that you need to learn, of course—but you've got to move on.

God wants you to move on!

I've said this in my first book, *Simplify and Live the Good Life*, and I'll say it again: Poverty is not simplicity. Poverty complicates life.

You see, we have a tendency to get stuck with trouble. It becomes our home. We get used to it.

I've always had this frustration of helping someone out of poverty, giving him a scholarship and even a new home... only to find out that after a few years, that same person will sabotage his life by getting someone pregnant, or marrying a bum, or committing a crime and ending up in jail... thereby going back to the poverty that he came from.

Why does he do this? Because in his subconscious mind, he's saying, "I'm poor and I'll always be poor." I realize that though I was able to "bring him out of the desert," he couldn't remove the desert from his heart, and so he kept on returning there.

Like the Israelites that had to fight Giants to enter the Promised Land, you too need to defeat tough Giants in your minds, and this terrible belief is one of them.

So say this with me: I'm going to the place of Simple Abundance.

Get comfortable with these words.

Anyone who doesn't believe in miracles isn't a realist.
—David Ben-Gurion

SECTION ONE

EXPECT MANNA IN THE DESERT

When the dew was gone, thin flakes like frost on the
ground appeared on the desert floor. When the Israelites
saw it, they said to each other, "What is it?" For they
did not know what it was. Moses said to them,
"It is the bread the Lord has given you to eat."
— Exodus 16:15

The Israelites walked through the desert for 40 years, and because of their lack, God had to feed them miraculously by giving them manna from the sky.

And in your life, when you go through the desert of your financial difficulty, the Lord provides you with miracles as well.

Through this manna, God teaches you a certain attitude to take with you, even when you are already living in the Promised Land.

Manna says, "Trust in Him totally."

Manna says, "Everything you have really comes from His hand."

Manna says, "Expect surprising miracles every day!"

Learn these lessons well.

Expect manna in the desert.

1

DEFINE SUCCESS IN YOUR OWN TERMS

Nothing is more simple than greatness;
indeed, to be simple is to be great.
—Ralph Waldo Emerson

When I was 13 years old, I looked like the perfect loser.

Because I wanted to imitate St. Francis of Assisi, I wore a crummy old tee-shirt, walked in cheap worn-out sandals, and had the muscular heft of a praying mantis. I never combed my hair or put on deodorant. Yet even at that time, I was already leading small prayer meetings, feeding the poor in the streets and having the time of my life.

I believe that in the eyes of God, this perfect loser was a great success.

When I was 20 years old, I didn't look as pathetic anymore. I learned that wearing presentable clothes and putting on deodorant made more people listen to my preaching—as the deodorant prevented them from fainting all the time. Though still penniless as the rat in my mother's kitchen, I was preaching from town to town, city to city, and country to country—bringing only God's love and my toothbrush with me.

And yes, I believe I was a great success as well.

Today, I'm still serving God with the same passion—preaching, writing, running dynamic organizations and pioneering new things for the Kingdom. I'm now married and have a family, and thus can no longer be penniless. I'm experiencing Simple Abundance and earning more than enough to be generous.

I know God thinks I'm a great success.

It's so easy to buy into the success gospel of the world. I'm not going to argue that success is important. But who says success has one definition?

Is success fat bank accounts, vacation houses, Rolexes and Jaguars?

Or is it a heart that loves and laughs and shares and cares?

Define success in your terms.

ACTION PLAN

Think. How do you define success? What are the things that should happen to you for you to say you're a great success? Write this down.

2
LEARN TO BE HAPPY WITHOUT LOTS OF MONEY

*Things that matter most must never be at
the mercy of things that matter least.*
—*Johann Wolfgang Von Goethe*

Money won't make you happy.

I don't care if you have a billion dollars, or maintain ten mansions across the globe, or wear diamonds the size of ping-pong balls or own 16 multinational corporations.

These things won't make you happy.

Here's my principle: Money will make you happy only if you have learned how to be happy without money!

If someone is miserable and says, "If I had enough money, then I'd be happy," I'd bet my life this person would continue to be miserable no matter how rich he got.

Best-selling author John Gray said, "Money is like a magnifying glass." I agree. If you're truly happy, money magnifies this feeling. It enlarges it. If you're miserable, money will make you even more miserable.

It's the same thing with marriage, or with a job, or with a house or with kids... A single person who is miserable and says, "If only I'd meet my perfect match and get married, then I'd be happy," is in for a big surprise. He'll be one very miserable married person. And worse, he'll make someone else as miserable as he is! Because the fact is obvious: Happy people make happy marriages.

This truth works with everything else, including money. You have to learn the secrets of true happiness before money comes, so that when it does come, you'll know how to handle it and become even happier.

Learn to be happy without lots of money.

ACTION PLAN

Think of five material things that you really craved for in the past that you now own. Examine your feelings. Are you now satisfied with what you have? Or do you now desire something n0ew to add or replace what you already have?

3
EVERYTHING YOU NEED TO BE HAPPY IS WITHIN YOU

*To love and be loved
is the greatest happiness of existence.*
—*Sydney Smith*

At the end of the day, there's only one thing that can make you happy.

It's called love.

A cliché? So what? It's the truth!

Because you're born for love.

You're designed for it. Every cell of your body, every part of your soul is created for love. I'm shouting it from the rooftops: Only love can make you truly happy!

Surround yourself with love. And practice it daily!

People in their deathbeds never say, "I wish I had bought a Ferrari," or "I wish I had spent more time in my office...." Listen to people in their dying hour and you'll hear the same regret: "I wish I had spent more time loving...."

I believe that relationships are the most important things in our lives—more important than all the wealth in the world.

By the way, how many of you have tried to quench your thirst with saltwater?

Don't bother trying. It doesn't work.

The only thing that saltwater does is make you even thirstier.

Money is like saltwater. No amount of money will quench your inner thirst for love and happiness. It'll only make you thirstier. You want more and more and more until you drop dead from spiritual malnutrition.

Learn to love every day!

Let this be your highest ambition in life: to be a great lover!

So when the money comes, you'll make money a servant of love.

Everything you need to be happy is within you.

ACTION PLAN

Are you a loving person? Are you kind, generous, forgiving? Do you love yourself too? Rate yourself from 1 to 10, with 10 being most loving. You'll notice that your score will also be your score for personal happiness.

Does your schedule and budget express the truth that your relationships are the most important things in the world?

4
LET MONEY MAKE YOU HOLY

Now he who supplies seed to the sower and bread for food
will also supply and increase your store of seed and will
enlarge the harvest of your righteousness.
—2 Corinthians 9:10

Yes, money can make you holier!

This can be a shock to some of you.

I've met people who say, "Earning too much money means I'll not be pleasing to God anymore."

I don't agree.

I believe that if you handle money the way God wants you to handle money, then it'll draw you closer to Him.

There's a big difference between saying, "I want to get rich for me!" and "I want to earn more, so that I can supply my needs and also supply the needs of the Kingdom!"

The gulf between these two is astronomical.

One will give you inner peace. The other, endless misery.

The latter will give you wings for your flight to heaven. The former? A special necklace with a ten-ton boulder as a pendant.

Personally, I made my choice a long time ago.

I want the wings!

I want to earn money and love God with every cent I have.

Because of these beliefs, for many years now, I give a lot of my income away, and have enormous joy doing so.

Friends, you have a choice.

You can let money make you evil and corrupt and selfish and miserable.

Or you can let money bring you closer to God and make you happy forever.

Let money make you holy.

ACTION PLAN

Has your money made you holier? Or has it made you the opposite? What specific things can you do to change this situation?

5
WORK YOUR SOUL, THEN YOUR WALLET

Wealth is not for spiritual neophytes;
they will be destroyed by it.
—Richard Foster

When money stops you from entering heaven, I recommend a drastic move: Give it up! It's better to enter heaven without money than have all the money in the world and end up in hell.

Remember: If your spiritual life can't handle the financial blessing, don't receive it. Because your spiritual life is the basis for your financial life.

Why? I believe a healthy spiritual life will make you faithful, loyal, humble, loving, honest and responsible—stuff you need for earning and managing your money.

For years, a friend of mine was struggling financially. She couldn't keep a stable job. I remember she even had to borrow money from me to attend our prayer meetings.

One day, her father was killed in an accident at work—and his company was partly at fault. Because the company was afraid of being sued, they offered my friend's family millions in an out-of-court settlement.

My friend was now awash with a sea of money! From someone who had no transportation money to attend a prayer meeting, she now drove a brand new car. Ironically, she stopped attending the prayer meeting because she said she was too busy starting her own business.

After two years, the business flopped, the car was sold, and all the money was gone.

My friend went back to begging for transportation money so that she could attend our prayer meetings again.

A sad story.

My friend's spiritual life simply wasn't ready for the money.

Work your soul, then your wallet.

ACTION PLAN

Will you be ready now if God were to start blessing you financially?

6
ASK GOD TO GIVE YOU MONEY

"Which of you fathers, if your son asks for a fish, will give him a snake instead? Or if he asks for an egg, will give him a scorpion?"
—Luke 11:11-12

For some people, the title above sounds blasphemous. But it's true.

If you don't believe it, then don't pray the "Our Father." Or at the very least, don't pray the middle line that says... "Give us each day our daily bread...."

God wants to provide for your needs.

Because He's Abba, the original Aramaic word used by Jesus for the "Our Father," which is better translated as "Our Daddy."

God is your Daddy. He wants to meet your needs— even material needs!

You know what our problem is?

We think we're more loving than God is.

As a father, I love giving stuff to my little boy. Whatever the tiny guy needs, I give. (Not his wants, just his needs.) It could be a new toy for him to throw all over the room for Daddy to "go fetch." It could be a Barney tee-shirt. It could be a 30-volume Biblical Hebrew-and-Greek Encyclopedia for his bedtime stories. Wow, the pleasure I feel merely watching him use it is much more than the pleasure he feels!

I just love giving him stuff he needs.

But some people think that God isn't that loving. They think that they have to bribe, beg, sacrifice and flagellate their backs to bloody pulp for God to give them what they need. That's lunacy! Then He wouldn't be Abba. He would simply be a monster who enjoys seeing us suffer.

Excuse me, but I'm not worshipping that God.

My God is Daddy. He loves, longs and leaps for joy whenever He has a chance to bless you.

Ask God to give you money.

ACTION PLAN

Pray the "Our Father" slowly. Pause a bit after you say, "Give us our daily bread." Tell Him what you mean by daily bread.

7

LIVE IN FIRST CLASS WHEREVER YOU ARE

Some pursue happiness… others create it.
—Anonymous

How do you begin your day?

I begin my day by saying, "This is a great day! Great blessings will come to me today!"

Because I believe we're prophets. And what we say happens.

If you wake up grumbling and say, "What bad luck will happen today?" that's what you'll get. Because the universe will deliver what you expect it to deliver.

Here's an example.

Because of my work, I take a lot of plane trips and I enjoy them.

Whenever the flight attendant gives me food, I think, "This comes from you, Lord." When I recline my seat, I say, "Wow! I can lean back and relax. Ahhhh!"

When they show a movie on the plane, I say, "What a treat!"

Some people don't ride the plane like that.

I see their eyes perennially looking towards the great divide between their section, which is economy, and the first class.

When the attendant serves their food in plastic plates, they say, "First class passengers get their food in porcelain with real silver cutlery."

And when they recline their seats, they grumble, "Only until here? In first class, seats adjust all the way to 180 degrees." And when the movie starts showing, they say, "In first class, they have a choice of 40 films in their personalized video."

This pathetic attitude doesn't only happen in planes.

It happens in life.

People go around living in houses and driving in cars and wearing clothes that they don't want because they perennially look for what they don't have.

As for me, I'm always in first class—no matter where I am!

Because in my book, there are no second class blessings. His love for me is first class. Always.

Live in first class wherever you are.

ACTION PLAN

Try it out tomorrow. When you wake up, jump out of bed and shout, "This is a great day. Great blessings will come to me today." And throughout the day, thank God for everything that you receive. You'll be surprised how different your day will be.

8

WORK ON THE LITTLE THAT YOU HAVE

When in doubt, don't buy it.
When in doubt, don't eat it.
When in doubt, don't marry him.
When in doubt, don't watch it.
When in doubt, throw it out.
—Connie Cox

Usually, our problem isn't God's lack of generosity but our lack of stewardship. Our problems aren't due to lack of money but to our mishandling of money.

Let me explain.

Let's say John and Carol buy an expensive car—a car beyond their budget. John and Carol are earning a combined income of P50,000 a month, but they buy a car worth P950,000. The monthly amortizations are killing them.

As they roll in their beds trying to get some sleep, they're filled with regret and say, "If only we were earning P100,000 a month! Then our problems would be solved."

I don't think so. Because if they were earning P100,000 a month, they would have bought a P950,000 car and a P200,000 home theater equipment, and a P5,000-a-month club membership, and a P50,000 stationary bike, and a P30,000 vacation in Palawan and…

Don't spend more than you can afford. Delay gratification! When I want to buy something, I ask three questions: First, "Will this give glory to God?"

If the answer is no, I don't buy it.

If yes, I ask the second question.

"Will this bless others?" It doesn't have to bless others directly. It can bless me, and thus bless others with a better me.

If the answer is no, I don't buy it.

If yes, I ask the third question: "Will you give this to me, Lord?"

Though I have the money to buy the item, I humor God to give it to me as manna. Usually, after a few months, I get it for free or at a greatly discounted price! Or I realize I didn't need that thing and thank God I didn't buy it impulsively.

I recall a friend complaining one day in June that she didn't have enough to pay for the kid's tuition. But I also knew that just six months before, she had bought a large-screen TV set—and was paying monthly installments for it. I also knew they had cable, and she was paying 500 pesos each month. That's P6000 a year! I asked her, "How can you not have anything to pay for the tuition this June when you had the money to buy the TV last January?"

She couldn't answer.

Work on the little that you have.

ACTION PLAN

Resolve never to borrow money or use credit for things that depreciate in value.

9
TRUST WHEN GOD SAYS NO

Whoever riseth from prayer a better man, his prayer is answered.
—George Meredith

Imagine your daughter one day telling you, "Mom, my graduation is approaching and I finished at the top of my batch."

"Yes, you did, honey," you smile proudly.

"So, I was thinking that being the great mother that you are, you would want to give me a special gift, because you love me and want to thank me for my sterling achievement," she says sweetly, as she wraps her arms around your waist. You feel like a huge anaconda is encircling you, but you dismiss the thought.

"Okaaaaay… And what gift would this be?" you say with a raised eyebrow.

"I was thinking of a car." And then your daughter cups your mouth and says, "But before you object, let me finish. Mom, it doesn't have to be brand-new. I'm not that unreasonable. A nice second-hand car will do for your Valedictorian daughter. What do you say, Mom?"

If you were that mother, would you give her the car? Some of you just might.

Well, what if I told you that she's only 12 and she's talking about her grade school graduation. Would you still give it to her?

Of course not. You'd tell her, "Over my dead body! Go ride your skateboard!"

No matter how much the anaconda pleads and cries buckets of tears in front of you, you'd still say "No." Why?

Because you love her.

God operates in the same way.

There'll be times when He won't grant you the money you're praying for if He knows it'll destroy the more important areas of your life.

You see, God isn't promising that you won't have seasons of need.

He isn't promising that you'll never have times when the budget is incredibly tight.

He isn't promising that you'll never have money problems.

This is His promise: that in all these trials, He guarantees His loyal, faithful, embracing Presence. He'll be beside you, holding your hand, throughout the journey in the desert. He'll never leave you.

Trust when God says "No."

ACTION PLAN

Close your eyes and thank God for the times He said "No" to you. Thank God when the answers to your prayers are delayed. He knows what He's doing.

10
CHOOSE SOUL SATISFACTION OVER PROSPERITY

All plenty which is not my God is poverty to me.
—St. Augustine

Imagine if one day the Almighty appeared before you in all His splendor and showed you two gifts. And then He says, "You can choose only one gift. In my left hand, I hold a box that contains 10 million dollars."

You begin to salivate and picture yourself in a world tour, sipping champagne in the first class cabin.

"In my right hand," God's booming voice interrupts your daydreaming, "I hold another box which contains something whose value you cannot measure." You're really excited. And then God says, "This box contains a sense of satisfaction."

Your jaw drops. You scratch your head.

Sense of satisfaction? What kind of animal is that?

God reads your mind and explains, "If you have a sense of satisfaction, you'll sleep soundly at night and you'll wake up refreshed every morning. You'll be free from anxiety and envy all throughout your life. You'll be content, no matter how simple and ordinary your life may be."

God asks, "Which would you choose?"

If you choose the 10 million dollars, let me tell you, you'll be making the most foolish decision in your life. For to be satisfied in your soul is far more valuable than all the wealth in the world. St. Paul says, "I know what it is to be in need, and I know what it is to have plenty. I have learned the secret of being content in any and every situation, whether well fed or hungry, whether living in plenty or in want."[3]

This is what I believe.

God promises us "soul satisfaction," not prosperity.

If we love God, prosperity may or may not come.

But soul satisfaction will.

Choose soul satisfaction over prosperity.

ACTION PLAN

Reflect on past moments in your life when you didn't have inner peace. Recall what caused this condition and learn lessons for the future.

11
TEACH YOUR KIDS THE LESSONS OF THE DESERT

I recall a story of a farmer who, when asked by his neighbor why he was working his sons so hard just to grow corn, replied, "I'm not just growing corn, I'm growing sons."
—*Kenneth Blanchard*

When God brings you to a financial desert, He's teaching you the most important lessons in life. Because the desert is God's university.

I know some parents who as kids were raised in poverty, but through struggle and faith, they've now left the financial desert. But here's the tragedy: Because they now have the ability to give a comfortable life to their children, they give too much of it.

If you're one of these parents, let me speak frankly to you. By giving everything that your children ask—expensive clothes, fancy toys, tiny cell phones—you rob them of the very thing that made you strong: the desert, the place where you struggled and built your character and made you who you are.

Don't give them everything they ask for.

Let them have the desert experience.

That's why I teach kids to think and talk in the language of the desert.

I tell them, "Don't ask your parents, 'Can I ask for P100?'"

Change your language. That's not the desert language.

The language of the desert is, "Mom, what can I do to earn P100?"

Maybe he can make and sell sandwiches in school, maybe he can invest in a candy machine, maybe he can sell insurance to the parents of his classmates, maybe he can tutor smaller children for a little fee, maybe….

As early as ten to 12 years old, teach your children to be entrepreneurs.

Teach your kids the lessons of the desert.

ACTION PLAN

If you're a parent, don't depend on your children's school to educate them financially. Most schools usually don't. You've got to do that on your own.

12
INSPIRE YOUR KIDS
TO LIVE SIMPLY

*Live your life so that your children
won't have to lie at your funeral.*
—Anonymous

Parents complain to me, "My kids are so materialistic!"

This is my answer. If you see your kids splurge on designer clothes, you can't complain if your closet is filled with these too. You've got to show the way.

Second, not only should you live simply, you should enjoy living simply. They won't see the logic if you give up your luxury car but hear you complain and bicker and fret about your second-hand car.

And when kids ask for expensive toys, expensive clothes and expensive cars, don't answer, "We can't afford it." That's a clear message that says, "We live a deprived life. Boo-hoo-hoo…" You have to clearly explain to them that living simply is a deliberate choice. Seat them before you and say, "Daddy and Mommy can buy that toy for you, but if we do, we'll have to work harder to earn money. Perhaps we won't come home for dinner and have to be away for the weekends. Do you want Daddy and Mommy to be away from you—or do you want them to always be here beside you?"

Don't expect it to sink in right away. Let them see you enjoy the simple things of life—not just those with a high price tag. In the end, a simple lifestyle is caught more than taught.

But here's one parent who had a kid that got the message and loved it.

> *It so happened that I was sitting and observing a group of boys, including my son, who sat in a circle nearby. Their conversation went like this: Child A: "My daddy is a doctor and he makes a lot of money and we have a swimming pool." Child B: "My daddy is a lawyer and he flies to Washington and talks to the president." Child C: "My daddy owns a company and we have our own airplane." Then my son (with aplomb, of course) looking proudly in my direction: "My daddy is here!"*
>
> —David Elkind

Inspire your kids to live simply.

ACTION PLAN
Share this book with your children who can already appreciate it.

13
THROW PARTIES FOR THE POOR

You can't live a perfect day without doing something for someone who will never be able to repay you.
—John Wooden

Eliza is my godmother.

And she sure knows how to throw a party.

One day, she went to the national women's prison and asked the warden, "Who are the women that have no visitors?" She was given a list of 20 inmates. Eliza started meeting them one by one, talking to them, most of the time listening, laughing at their stories, crying at their heartaches. Later on, when she learned that one needed laundry soap, that would be her gift on her next visit. Sometimes it would be a toothbrush. A pair of slippers. A little cheesecake. But her most expensive gift was still her presence. She would go there regularly, as a friend.

No big plans. No great projects.

Loving the poor can be something really small.

But it has to be constant, until it becomes a way of life.

When you're about to throw a party, what kind of "guest list" would Jesus recommend? Again, His crazy favoritism shows. He says, "Don't bring in the best and the brightest. Don't invite those with silk ties and brand new cars and jewels and cell phones. Call those who can't eat three decent meals a day. Call in as well those who are abandoned: the mentally insane, the physically handicapped, the orphan, the widow, the drug addict, the drunkard, the sinner...."

Because it's going to be a Party of God's love.

Our lives—each conversation we hold, each encounter we have, each act we do—should be a celebration of God's extravagant love for the outcast.

Throw parties for the poor.

ACTION PLAN

When was the last time you did something for someone, knowing that someone could never repay you?

If possible, do a good deed secretly. Don't even let the recipient know from whom the good deed came. You'll be pleased at the inner peace that you will have.

14
LIVE FOR ETERNAL RICHES

Do not store up for yourselves treasures on earth, where moth
and rust destroy, and where thieves break in and steal.
But store up for yourselves treasures in heaven.
—Matthew 6:19-20

David Myers, in his book *The Pursuit of Happiness,* gives the testimony of his friend Ruth, a nurse who worked in a Nigerian village. She recalls "…a group of five- to seven-year-old boys wearing rags for clothes and racing along our compound's driveway with a toy truck made of tin cans from my trash. They had spent the greater part of a morning engineering the toy—and were squealing with delight as they pushed it with a stick. My sons, with Tonka trucks parked under their beds, looked on with envy."

Because the Tonka truck isn't better than the tin truck.

The brand new car isn't better than the second-hand car.

Yes, we do need the basics of life: basic food, basic housing, basic clothing. No one argues that a starving beggar on the street isn't happy.

But once our basic needs are met, wealth gives diminishing returns of pleasure.

Your second million pesos won't taste as good as your first million.

Why? Because once we're physically comfortable, our souls start manifesting hunger pangs. We start longing for heaven.

Here's a powerful spiritual principle: Everything in your life is negotiable to God.

Your wealth. Your health. Your security. There's only one thing that's non-negotiable to Him: your soul. That means the Lord will take away your wealth, your health, your security—if that is the only way to bless your soul.

But if blessing you with wealth, health, and security will bless your soul, then He will do that. I've experienced the financial blessings of God in my life. They're for real!

But they're not His priority.

His priority is that You live forever.

Make that your priority as well.

Live for eternal riches.

ACTION PLAN

Every good deed you do is a deposit you make to your heavenly account. What do you think is the status of this heavenly account?

> *There is nothing to fear but fear itself.*
> —*Franklin D. Roosevelt*

SECTION TWO

DEFEAT THE GIANTS

> *"We explored the land and found it to be rich and fertile...*
> *But the people who live there are powerful... Even worse,*
> *we saw the descendants of the giants there."*
> —*Numbers 13:27-28*

I believe that every day I'm surrounded with the blessings of God.

You and I are swimming in a sea of blessing, and we don't know it!

Every day, I live with this core belief: I'll receive abundant blessing from God today. Because I'm convinced that God is a blesser. Twenty-four hours a day, He thinks of ways to bless me.

Imagine how that core belief shapes the kind of day I'll have! I may actually have more problems than the person next to me, but that belief alone can change the way I look at those problems.

That's how powerful beliefs are!

Sometimes though, our beliefs are dead wrong. But they are powerful nonetheless, and they can prevent God's blessings from flowing into our lives.

That's why I call these wrong beliefs Giants.

And Giants will always block your way towards the Promised Land.

Another kind of Giant is the wrong motives we have for earning money.

If you earn money with wrong motives, you work with stress, you act with disquiet and chaos. Oh yes, you may succeed. But at what price? Because selfishness is not a great friend. It'll eat you up and destroy you inch by inch, cell by cell.

Saturate your mind with the right motives for earning money. Let these be the fuel that drives every business decision, the driving force behind every money-making project.

This is what happens when you know that you're earning money for the right motives: You're at peace with yourself, you're in synch with the universe, you're moving under the power of God.

Defeat the Giants.

1
BELIEVE THAT YOUR BLESSING ACCOUNT IS FULL

If God seems far away, guess who moved!
—Fr. John Hampsch

Imagine if one day I ask for your bank account number. And you give it to me. The next day, I phone you and tell you, "I've deposited one million dollars in your bank account."

Naturally, you'd laugh and say, "Sure, Bo. Thaaaaaaaanks. That's a good one." You'd hang up and forget our conversation. Why? Because you know—it's a core belief that's pretty set in cement—that I don't have the capacity to give you one million dollars.

But let's just imagine that I really did put a million dollars in your bank account. (Let's say I robbed a few banks the day before and didn't know where to hide the money.)

Here's my question: Would you benefit from the million in your account?

No you wouldn't.

Unless you believe that I really gave you a million dollars—and withdrew it.

Here's my core belief, and it's pretty set in cement too: I believe that God has deposited zillions of Heaven's resources to your Blessing Account.

You've got all the love and joy and peace and wisdom and holiness and—yes, finances—that you need in this world to serve Him and live a happy life.

But much of these zillions of blessings are unclaimed!

Why? Because of the Giant in your mind that says, "There are no blessings. God won't bless me."

A person who says that can't see the beauty of the sunrise or the drizzle of the soft rain as the Lord's gifts to him. It wouldn't even enter his mind that his friends and family are fantastic expressions of God's love for him.

Defeat this Giant and withdraw from your Blessing Account.

Remember: God created the entire universe for you—a universe of blessings that are only waiting to be claimed!

Believe that your Blessing Account is full.

ACTION PLAN

Watch the Discovery Channel. And see how extravagant God is! For example, he could have created just one planet—earth. Why an entire solar system? And He could have made one solar system—ours. Why billions of them in our galaxy, the Milky Way? And why billions of galaxies in this universe? And are we sure there's only one universe?

It's His reckless generosity at work. That's the God that you're dealing with!

2
BELIEVE THAT YOU CAN ATTRACT MONEY

Our greatest dreams are never out of reach,
only out of belief.
—Wayne Dyer

If I focus on love, hang around with very loving people, read inspiring books of saints who loved greatly, you can be sure I'll attract a lot of love in my life.

But if I focus on my deep hurts, talk with other bitter people who like recounting their own hurts, watch movies about revenge, what do you think will I attract?

I repeat: You attract what you focus on.

You've got the ability to attract anything in your life.

Love. Peace. Joy. Wisdom. Happiness. Even money!

So if you want to attract money, you've got to focus on money.

Read about money. Be financially literate. Hang around people who are financially wise. Talk with small-time entrepreneurs, especially those who've learned from their failures. Sell something. Start a tiny business. And never give up no matter how many times you fail.

Believe that you can attract money.

ACTION PLAN

Who are the people that you hang around with? What kind of conversations do you have? What kind of books do you read? What kind of movies do you watch? Remember that you'll attract what you focus on.

3
BELIEVE THAT POVERTY ENDS WITH YOU

Change your attitude and your actions at the same time
and you can have anything you want.
— Anne Hartley

I've heard people say this line, "I'll probably be poor for the rest of my life." That statement is so powerful, it will influence their future and become their reality! Because beliefs are self-fulfilling prophecies.

Leny is another woman I met who always talked about how poor her family was. "My parents are poor. My grandparents are poor. All my relatives are poor. *Pati aso at pusa namin, mahirap.*[5] I myself am very poor and will probably be poor for the rest of my life."

My heart goes out to Leny and her family—and people like them. Because poverty has become their family identity, it'll be very difficult for them to detach themselves from this terribly wrong belief.

Oh, if only they knew that it is this belief that is keeping them poor!

We had a house helper that had another core belief. Helen[6] came from a tiny fishing island in the Visayas, and her family was even poorer than Leny's family. But somewhere in her heart of hearts, she believed that poverty didn't run through her veins. Helen believed that this family inheritance of poverty could stop right there with her! So even as she cooked our meals and cleaned our house during the day, she went to classes at night. After she finished high school and college, we bade her farewell and she began working immediately as a lowly office clerk.

Today, our former house helper is now a manager earning P50,000 a month! Let me say it again: Our core beliefs are self-fulfilling prophecies that determine the future of our lives!

Believe that poverty ends with you.

ACTION PLAN

Say this with conviction. "God will bless me financially." Say these words every day. Until you become comfortable with them in your very gut.

4

BELIEVE THAT MONEY IS EVERYWHERE

The Lord will grant you abundant prosperity…
The Lord will open the heavens, the storehouse of his bounty,
to send rain on your land in season and to bless all the work
of your hands. You will lend to many nations but will borrow
from none.
—Deuteronomy 28:11-12

When I was growing up, I remember my mother telling me thousands of times, "Money doesn't grow on trees, Bo."

This is called a scarcity mentality.

I'll give you an example.

Some people believe that there's very little money out there. That the Danding Conjuangcos and the Lucio Tans and the Henry Sys have cornered it all for themselves and there's nothing left for us.

If you believe that, then that belief will be true for you. You'll really have a hard time earning money! It becomes true because your mind will subconsciously exert effort to prove it true!

Today, I don't have a scarcity mentality.

I now believe that money grows on trees!

Because I operate on an abundance mentality.

All the money I need for life is out there, all around me.

I'm swimming in an ocean of blessing.

If I utilize the talents that God has given to me, and pay the price of hard work required by success, the money I need will come flowing in.

Here's the truth…

Believe that money is easy to find, and the world will prove it to you.

Believe that money is very difficult to find, and the world will prove it to you.

It really all depends on you.

So what should you do?

Believe that money is everywhere.

ACTION PLAN

Do you believe that money grows on trees?

Start being open to the money out there. Write down some ideas how you can earn the money that is all around you. No idea is too wild. Pray for this list.

5
DON'T AVOID WEALTH

There are no limits to the mind
except those that we acknowledge.
—Napoleon Hill

I know someone who is always sick. She always has a cold, a cough or some pain. We start talking one day and soon, I find out why. Because when she's sick, that's the only time she receives a lot of attention and love and concern. When she's well, she doesn't receive attention and love and concern! She keeps getting sick because her subconscious mind tells her body to get sick.

This is what psychology calls the phenomenon of secondary gain. The secondary gain of getting sick was getting her attention and love from others.

And so here's one reason why some people avoid wealth—even if on the outside they seem to be looking for it, the secondary gain is getting attention and love from those that help them.

Billy is one such person. He has been poor all his life. He has been a parasite since he was a kid, well trained by his own parents who were also parasites. So he can't find a regular job. He constantly shows up at relatives' homes because his electricity is being cut off or his landlord is kicking him out of the house. Sound familiar?

Deep within Billy, you'll find someone who feels loved when other people help him in his need.

To know if you have the Parasite Complex, ask yourself, "Do I subconsciously fear financial independence because it will cause other people not to help me anymore? Do I feel most loved when I receive financial help from others?"

Don't avoid wealth.

ACTION PLAN

Imagine one year from now how you will be helping others through the financial blessings God will give you. Close your eyes. Think about it. Visualize it. Feel that joy of generosity.

6

DON'T TRY TO CONTROL YOUR REPUTATION, ONLY YOUR INTEGRITY

Make it your ambition to lead a quiet life,
to mind your own business and to work with your hands…
—1 Thessalonians 4:11

Here's another Giant blocking your entrance to the Promised Land.

Some people have this subconscious belief: "People will think bad of me if I become rich." Insane? You can't imagine how many people have this conviction.

If you have this belief, you'll subconsciously avoid wealth—no matter how you outwardly try to gain it.

For example, I've met some lay Christian workers who feel they have to continue to be poor so that people will respect them. Because if they're not poor, then people might accuse them of using Church funds.

But this is crazy. The truth is, we're never in control of our reputation—only our integrity.

According to one study made in the University of the Philippines, an 18 year old person knows an average of 263 persons. And the older you get, the more people you know.

That means you have 263 different reputations or more! Try controlling that.

But you only have one integrity, and that's what you can control.

If your conscience is clear and God is cheering you, then no matter what other people say, live your life! Don't stop for every dog that barks on the road.

Don't try to control your reputation—only your integrity.

ACTION PLAN

Are you holding back what you want to do because you fear what other people will say? Even if you know that what you'll be doing is God's will? Stop delaying His work.

7
DON'T BELIEVE THAT ALL RICH PEOPLE ARE CHEATS

Command them [the rich] to do good, to be rich in good deeds, and to be generous and willing to share.
—1 Timothy 6:18

Some people think that rich people are evil and poor people are holy.

Why do they think this way? Because they believe that God favors the poor. And I agree! But the reason He makes them His favorites is to rescue them from poverty, not to keep them there. So what happens if they're rescued and are no longer poor? Do they automatically become evil?

Some people think that if you're earning too much money, you're automatically evil. That's not true. Earning too much money may mean that God is lending you a lot more money so you could help the poor. He's merely using you as his conduit of blessings.

Why am I particular about how you view the rich?

Because this is a Giant that will prevent you from entering your Promised Land.

This is how this Giant works:

If you believe that all rich people are corrupt, crooks and cheats—you wouldn't want to be one, right? So subconsciously, you'll find a way to avoid wealth. It's that simple.

So examine how you view the rich.

Do you resent them for being rich?

Do you envy them for being where they are?

Do you feel that they're devious people?

Shun these thoughts—because these are the very thoughts that prevent financial blessings from flowing into your life!

Don't believe that all rich people are cheats.

ACTION PLAN

Read about rich people in the Bible who followed God. For example, Abraham, Joseph of Arimathea and the women of influence who supported Jesus and His disciples.

8
SELL YOURSELF
TO YOURSELF FIRST

The most important opinion you have is the one you have
of yourself. And the most important conversation you'll have
is the one you'll have with yourself.
—Zig Ziglar

Joe Girard is described by the *Guinness Book of World Records* as the Greatest Car Salesman in the world. While every other car salesman sold seven cars a month, he sold six cars a day. And if you think he did this by selling a fleet of cars to companies, think again. He sold one car to one customer every single day—face to face, belly to belly.

How did he do it?

If you ask him, Joe will give you this answer: He didn't sell cars. He sold Joe Girard. Because the only reason why people bought cars from him was if they first believed and trusted him. So he had to sell himself first.

But if he was going to make others believe in him, he needed to believe in himself first. In other words, if he was going to sell himself, then he had to be his first buyer!

Every morning, after he combed his hair and put on his shoes and donned his coat, he looked into the mirror and asked himself the question, "Would I buy me?"

In other words, did he believe that he could do it? That God had given him the ability to make people happy by selling them good cars—and in the process earn money?

I'm convinced that this is the first secret of financial success.

You have to believe that God has gifted you with all the abilities that you need in order to earn more than enough.

Sell yourself to yourself first.

ACTION PLAN

Before you leave the house every morning, first answer the question, "Would I buy me?" If the answer is no, don't leave the house. Find out why. Get rid of the doubts and start marketing yourself to yourself again. Leave the door only when you're totally sold on yourself—that you're a great product you'll be proud to share with others.

9
PURIFY YOUR MOTIVES

We have met the enemy and he is us.
—Pogo

One day, the Pope died and went to heaven. St. Peter embraced him and said, "Because your motives for preaching have always been pure, here's your BMW."

As the good Pope drove his shiny BMW through the golden roads, he met a Cardinal driving a Toyota Corolla. Both alighted from their cars and greeted each other. The Cardinal explained his cheaper car. "St. Peter said I sometimes had impure motives when I preached. Aside from spreading God's Word, I also wanted to become famous."

While they talked, they saw a familiar face—a Bishop— driving a Kia Pride. After greeting each other, the Bishop said, "I'm embarrassed to tell you both, but St. Peter said that I sometimes had impure motives when I preached: I wanted to be famous and," he gushed, "I also wanted girls to fall in love with me."

After talking some more, the three men saw another person coming: Bo Sanchez—riding a rusty bicycle. Upon greeting him, the three asked, "Goodness, Bo, why are you riding a bike?" Bo sighed and said, "St. Peter said I had impure motives when I preached. I wanted to become famous and," he gushed, "I wanted guys to fall in love with me!"

The story above is entirely fictional but the point I wish to drive home isn't: that motives play a big role in the eyes of God.

We can do something very good in our eyes and in the eyes of men, but if our motives are wrong—they don't mean much before the eyes of God.

Here's the second thing that motives do: They determine our state of personal happiness and inner peace.

Do you want to feel inner peace today? Twenty-four hours a day and seven days a week? The answer is radically simple. Let your motives be coherent with your inner conscience. In other words, do everything—and by everything, I mean everything—with pure motives! Work, pray, play, drive, cook, serve, eat, exercise, talk, rest and love with pure motives. If your motives go against your deepest values as held by your conscience, you will feel scattered and divided as a person.

And especially when it comes to making money.

Here are the *wrong* motives for earning money:

So people will like you.

To feel secure.

And here are the *right* ones:

To provide for your family.

To enjoy material things as expressions of God's love.

To enjoy work.

To love extravagantly.

Purify your motives.

ACTION PLAN

Examine your motives for making money. Why do you want more money? Write down your answers. Are you at peace with these answers?

10
DON'T USE MONEY SO PEOPLE WILL LIKE YOU

Money can't buy you friends.
Your enemies just treat you a little bit better.
— Anonymous

My friend was telling me her embarrassing experience at a wedding reception for the rich and famous. She noticed that the people around her table had the smallest, cutest, tiniest cell phones in the universe.

And that was when her own cell phone rang.

"Darn," she groaned. When she retrieved the massive phone from her bag, her seatmate whispered to her, "I like your phone. Tell me, have you registered that thing with the Armed Forces of the Philippines?"

That day, my friend vowed to buy herself a newer and smaller cell phone.

But I told her that if the only reason she wanted to have a new phone was so that she could "fit in" with her friends, that wasn't a very noble motive. On the other hand, if she were developing varicose veins on her arm because of carrying her cell phone around, that would be another matter. I added, "But if you see your phone as body building equipment, then don't bother. Use it with confidence!"

Because some of the most insecure people I've met are very rich individuals who own 17 homes. They feel naked when they don't wear their jewelry.

I'll say it again. To feel worthy is a matter of loving yourself and allowing God to love you—accepting yourself as wonderful and special and beautiful.

Don't use money so people will like you.

ACTION PLAN

Every time you feel that a certain crowd doesn't accept you, leave for a while. Close your eyes and ask yourself, "Do I like me? Do I accept myself?"

If the answer is yes, go back to that crowd with confidence. You don't need their acceptance to exist there. Be happy!

If the answer is no, then there lies your problem. Fix it.

11
DON'T USE MONEY TO FEEL SECURE

When money talks, it often merely says, "Goodbye."
—Poor Richard Jr.

Last month, I was watching *Larry King Live* on CNN. He was interviewing Ted Turner, the man who runs and owns much of CNN. At the end of the interview, Larry King asked the multi-millionaire Ted Turner, "What does it feel like not to worry about money?"

I was taken aback by his answer, and so was Larry King. Turner said, "I do worry about money a lot."

These words come from someone who is probably wealthier than 99.999% of the population of the world. Yes, he still worries about money!

We will never reach a point when we will have so much money that we won't worry about it anymore. Because the solution to worry isn't a certain level of financial wealth—but a certain level of trust in the Lord—that He cares for us more than we can ever imagine!

Don't use money to feel secure.

ACTION PLAN

What are your deepest fears? Surrender them to God now.

12
MAKE MONEY TO PROVIDE FOR YOUR FAMILY

If anyone does not provide for his relatives,
and especially for his immediate family,
he has denied the faith and is worse than an unbeliever.
—1 Timothy 5:8

My favorite saint is Francis of Assisi. I tell people to imitate his fervent love for God, his desire for prayer, his gentle care for creation. But I've now realized that if you want to imitate St. Francis in his level of simplicity—which was poverty—be sure you're not married. Because if you are, and you still follow his poverty lifestyle, I believe you're committing sin. A very serious sin!

It also makes us very miserable.

> *Celibacy is not essential to simplicity, but it is*
> *essential to some expressions of simplicity. If we*
> *want to live like Francis (of Assisi), we had better*
> *not be married. If we want to be married, we had*
> *better not try to live like Francis. The failure to*
> *understand this simple fact has caused a great deal of*
> *misery in human society.*
>
> *—Richard Foster*

Once in a while, I meet a married man who tells me he heard the Lord call him to leave his job and serve Him fully. My first question to him will always be, "Has God also told you how you are going to financially support your family?"

Usually, they say something like, "No, but I believe He will provide." That's when I get nervous. Eight times out of ten, I find out that they've heard wrongly. God wasn't talking to them at all. All they heard was their confused desire to sincerely serve the Lord—mixed with wrong theology, impulsive emotions and even a hidden desire to escape their problems.

Some of them, however, do hear a genuine call from the Lord. And usually, the Christian worker gains a supportive community of people around them who will commit to provide for their financial needs, regularly. Because his kids eat regularly as well! When this happens, it works very well.

I've said it before and I'll say it again: For someone who is married and has kids, poverty isn't the simple lifestyle. Poverty complicates life!

Make money to provide for your family.

ACTION PLAN
Does your level of simplicity fit with your status? If you're married, is your expression of simplicity an expression of love for your spouse and children? Have a meeting with your spouse and make these decisions together.

13

MAKE MONEY TO ENJOY MATERIAL THINGS AS EXPRESSIONS OF GOD'S LOVE

*Command those who are rich in this present world not to be arrogant nor to put their hope in wealth, which is so uncertain, but to put their hope in God, who richly provides us with everything for our **enjoyment**.*
—1 Timothy 6:17 (emphasis added)

This may be a shock to some of you.

But I believe this is a very pure motive for earning money: to enjoy material things as expressions of God's love.

Material things should be received as God's gifts, as tokens of affection from a loving Father. And when you see material things from this perspective, you don't need expensive stuff to give you a high. The simplest things delight you because you know they come from a loving God. *Magiging mababaw ang kaligayahan mo* .7

Let me share with you something mushy.

I actually love my old car.

My car has no power locks, power windows, power speakers or power seats. It's uh… powerless.

But every morning, whenever I ride my car, I get a thrill in my heart. A sense of peace overcomes me. I sit in the driver's seat, pause for a while, touch the dashboard and breathe in the affection of God for me. And then I whisper, "Thank You for your love!" I know it sounds corny, but I'd rather be corny and happy than sophisticated and miserable.

Contentment for me means insisting on the best, and I insist that I get it.

So I insisted that I get the best car in the world—and I did.

Some of you who have seen my old junk may object and say, "Bo, you've got to be kidding. When you say 'best car,' you mean a Jaguar or BMW. Not your wreck."

I disagree. A BMW can't compare with my lovely old car.

Let me give you three reasons.

First, imagine if I'm driving my ol' beauty and beside me a BMW drives by. And then on the next corner, a kidnapper is watching both of us, wondering which one of us he'd kidnap. Guess who he's going to choose, hmm?

Second, I can park my car anywhere without any fear. Even with the windows open. Because the thief will take one look at it and turn away in disgust.

And here's the third reason why I believe my car is the best car in the world.

In Manila traffic, no matter what you do, your car will get nicked, nudged, scratched, scraped and bumped. Two months ago, that's just what happened. I was driving on the hi-way when this other car scraped my left side.

I looked at his car and saw it was old.

The other driver looked at my car and saw it was old as well.

We smiled at each other, waved and drove off.

Now imagine if I drove a BMW?

I'd have to get off, scream at the top of my lungs, "It's your fault!" and argue with the other driver for two hours, snarl Manila traffic into a standstill and have a possible heart attack.

Honestly, I don't have the time or energy for something like that.

I love my car.

It's God's love made material.

Make money to enjoy material things as expressions of God's love.

ACTION PLAN

What are the simple pleasures that you can afford? Make a list. Relish in them. Bask in them. Thank God for His love!

14
MAKE MONEY AND ENJOY YOUR WORK

A musician must make music, an artist must paint,
a poet must write, if he is to be ultimately at peace with himself.
— Abraham Maslow

I love my work!

I love writing and preaching and composing songs. I get a high when I see an empty computer screen in front of me. It beckons to me, "Write something!" Ooooh, I just love that sensation.

I know that some people would find me extremely weird, but waves of pleasure flow through me when I actually have spare time to read a good book and do some research. But why am I like this?

Because before history began a billion years ago, God already wanted me to be a writer and preacher and a songwriter. Thus, He prepared me and gave me the raw materials for this kind of work.

On the other hand, I can't imagine myself as an accountant. I can only guess that on my second day as an accountant, I'd still be balancing books, but I'd already be doing it in Pavilion C, third floor, National Mental Hospital.

Medicine is out of the question. I'd probably faint if my patient said "Ouch."

Engineering would be too exact a science for me. I'd probably build bridges that curve, twist and curl up for no apparent reason except that they look nice.

Law? The mention of the word makes me feel dizzy.

I'm made for preaching and writing and composing songs, period.

Examine your work: Do you feel you "fit" in your career?

Do you enjoy it and see that God made you for it?

Pray for this grace!

Make money and enjoy your work.

ACTION PLAN

Follow the trail of His anointing. If God is blessing you in that endeavor, if you're meeting small successes, these are small guide lights that direct you to your destiny. Move in that direction.

15
MAKE MONEY TO LOVE EXTRAVAGANTLY

*"I will make you into a great nation and I will bless you;
I will make your name great, and you will be a blessing...
all peoples on earth will be blessed through you."*
—Genesis 12:2-3

Earn money so you can be generous to the work of the
Lord and to the poor.

And earn money so you can be generous with your
loved ones.

Living a simple life doesn't mean being stingy!

Mary, the sister of Martha, anointed Jesus with
expensive ointment worth 300 days wages. Now that's
extravagant! Judas Iscariot complained that the perfume
should have been sold off and given to the poor.[8] Jesus,
however, didn't think it was wasteful but rather praised
Mary's act of love.

The point? Once in a while, we can be excessive when it
comes to giving gifts to one another—out of love.

When my father celebrated his 80th birthday, I recall my
family spent a small fortune for an expensive dinner where
we invited all his friends. (Well actually, it wasn't that
expensive. At 80 years old, most of his friends were

already chatting with St. Peter.) Some would have accused us of being "excessive" because what we spent during that birthday party could have fed ten families in Bangladesh for an entire month. But somehow, I knew that God was smiling when we did that for Dad.

It may have been excessive if as a family we didn't regularly share our belongings with the poor. But that is something we have done all our lives, thanks to my father's inspiring example.

One day, I bought Holland tulips for my wife. Again, a part of me was saying that I could feed lunch to ten orphans from Nigeria with what I spent. But I felt God assure me that He wanted me to be loving towards my wife—and that He provide me with more wealth so that I can help the orphans on another occasion.

Make money to love extravagantly.

ACTION PLAN

Who should you love extravagantly? Make plans and put them in your calendar.

The harder I work, the luckier I get.
—James Thurber

SECTION THREE

WORK THE PROMISED LAND

The manna stopped falling then, and the Israelites no longer had any. From that time on they ate food grown in Canaan.
Joshua 5:12

One day, a friend of mine who tithes regularly complained that he wasn't getting financially blessed. He was still barely making ends meet.

I told him, "Tithing is one principle of financial blessing. Are you following the other principles of financial blessing?"

He stared at me amazed. "Other principles? I only know one and that's tithing."

I rattled off my list. "Do you live a simple life? Do you tame your materialistic desires? Do you avoid credit? Do you believe that God has given you all the abilities that you need in order to earn more than enough? Do you work hard? Do you persevere when you fail repeatedly? Do you serve your customers with love and excellence?"

He shook his head.

My friend confessed that he's an impulsive buyer and uses his credit card recklessly. He never saves. He never opens himself to new income streams.

Many people want to succeed but they're not willing to pay the price of success.

As much as I love manna and the supernatural miracles of God, let me say it again: Manna is designed by God to teach you an **attitude**, not a behavior.

Mixing up these two words has caused untold misery in people's lives.

If you think manna is teaching you a behavior, you'll say hilarious things like... "Don't budget. God will just miraculously work it all out." or "Don't save, don't buy insurance, don't think of investments or dabble into business. That's all worldly stuff and will bring you to hell. Just trust God."

If you say those things, you'll never leave the desert of financial difficulty.

Do you want to be successful in life?

Success in biblical language is "bearing fruit."

But God doesn't give you the fruit of success. What He gives you instead is the land that will bear the fruit of success.

So in the Promised Land, you need to work that land: till the soil, plant the seeds and harvest the crops. A lot of hard, back-straining work!

My friend, in the Promised Land you decide how much money you want to earn.

Work the Promised Land.

1
TILL THE SOIL OF YOUR MIND

The single most powerful asset we have is our mind.
If it is trained well, it can create enormous wealth
in what seems to be an instant.
—Robert Kiyosaki

Wealth comes from your mind.

If you want to reach the place of Simple Abundance, till the soil of your mind.

You need to prepare your thinking for financial blessings.

I believe that many receive wealth—and lose it quickly—because they didn't till the soil of their minds.

What do I mean?

Increase your knowledge and financial literacy.

Develop your financial vocabulary. Find out what cash flow, inflation, assets, stocks, pension funds and mutual funds mean. Study. Attend seminars. Read books. Talk to small businessmen. Look for mentors.

Start a tiny business. When you get bankrupt, start another one.

Sell something. Anything! Even if talking to a stranger makes you faint. The education you'll get is phenomenal.

And never give up, no matter how many times you fail.

And then the miracle will happen: When your mind is ready, the opportunities come.

For example, I'm planning to invest in the real estate business next year.

Do I have oodles of cash right now? No, I don't.

But that doesn't prevent me from reading books, attending seminars and talking to real estate people. Anyway, these seminars don't ask me how much money I have! So I sit there and people think I'm some rich dude with cash to burn.

They don't know I'm just gaining an education—for free.

You see, a lot of people get burned in business because they're trigger-happy. When they see an enticing opportunity, they quickly grab their life savings and dump it in right away. Of course the odds for failure are great!

Here's something I learned from the Gurus of the Real Estate business: Don't buy a house or condo or property until you've seen 100 sites.

Wow. That's a lot of tilling the soil.

Use that principle in other areas of making money as well.

Till the soil of your mind.

ACTION PLAN

What jobs or businesses are you interested in? Write them down. Next, list the resources that are available to you: books, seminars and experts in the field. Start tilling!

2
PLANT YOUR SEEDS

You must be good in either two things:
Planting in the spring or begging in the fall.
—Jim Rohn

Let me tell you my story.

From the day I started preaching at the age of 13 until I reached the age of 30, I didn't know anything about savings, investments or business. You see, I thought God wanted me to live a single life, either as a priest or as a lay celibate. So why think of money when I could live on the sidewalk? I was totally focused on serving God. I was so busy preaching, writing, pioneering and doing the craziest things for the Lord.

When I was 30, I felt God calling me to get married.

Suddenly, I realized I had to earn money, save money and think of my future.

And when I set about doing that, I realized one thing: Earning money was sooooo easy! Let me tell you why: Because for almost 20 years, I was planting seeds. I was constantly learning new skills—whether it was public speaking, or events management, or touch typing, or selling something or planning. I was also developing my personality. I was building my confidence. I was organizing my network.

Let me give you an example of what I mean.

Since the age of 13, I have been composing worship songs for God. I did this because I simply loved singing for Him. I didn't know I was planting seeds.

Recently, a friend called me up and said he was in a tight fix. He said he was making an ad campaign and he needed an advertisement jingle in two days!

So I sat down, got my guitar, made a jingle and gave it to him. Much of the song was finished in an hour.

My friend called me up later to tell me how much I had earned.

I couldn't believe my ears. That amount of money for an hour's work?

But that's because for 20 years, I was planting seeds.

Plant your seed.

ACTION PLAN

Look for growth opportunities that need your service. Volunteer to serve without thinking of a return or profit.

3
KEEP SOME SEED FOR THE NEXT PLANTING SEASON

Divide your portion to seven, or even to eight,
for you do not know what misfortune may occur on the earth.
—Ecclesiastes 11:2

At harvest, keep some seed for next planting.

In other words, each time you get your salary, set aside an amount for the future.

The best advice I can give you is Jim Rohn's 70/30 Rule. Here's what it means:

First, you've got to learn how to live on 70% of your income.

I can hear your objections now. (Howling protest, really.) "Bo, I can't live on 70% of my income! You must be insane!"

Exactly.

Be insane. Be ruthless. Simplify like crazy.

This is your future we're talking about.

And here's what you'll do with the rest of the 30%:

> First, give 10% to God.
> Second, give 10% for your retirement.
> Third, give 10% for creating assets.

I'll discuss each of these in the next three chapters.

Keep some seed for the next planting season.

ACTION PLAN

How do you live on 70% of your income? For many of us, we don't have an income problem; we have a spending problem. Track your spending. Get into a Seven-Day Spending Diagnosis. For seven days, before leaving for work, tuck in your pocket a little notebook where you can jot down expenses every time you purchase something. This "diagnosis" will give you the wisdom where to cut back and do some "radical surgery."

4
GIVE 10% TO GOD

To tithe is to trust. It is to acknowledge that God will provide,
that God will protect. When you give to God you create an
investment in your own spirituality, your community,
your family and your faith.
—Judith Briles

Make your ten percent to God your first expense.[9] The moment you receive your salary, set ten percent aside and give it to the Lord. Believe me, if you won't make it your first expense, you'll never be able to do it.

Some people say, "I can't tithe now. Perhaps when my income gets bigger…"

Some will even add, "Bo, I'll give half of my lotto winnings when I win the P100 million prize. I'm giving P50 million to the Lord. That's a promise!"

But I tell them, "If you can't give your P50 now, you won't be able to give your P50 million tomorrow." Because he who's faithful in small things will be faithful in big things, but he who isn't faithful in small things won't be faithful in big things.

Why do we give ten percent to God?

Because you want to love Him with your wealth.

And you want to be blessed beyond your wildest dreams.

Why do you get blessed? That's just how the universe is rigged. You reap what you sow. You'll end up receiving far more than what you have given to God.

Here's another thing. I've had the pleasure of reading secular books on personal finance. Somewhere in the last chapters of these books, I discovered something fascinating: These secular authors recommend tithing! I couldn't believe it. No, they don't tell you to do it because you need to obey God. They tell their readers to tithe because it creates an abundance mentality and delivers them from scarcity mentality—a very critical step to being financially successful.

Give ten percent to God.

ACTION PLAN

When's your next payday? Have a tithe envelope ready. Make a decision where God wants you to give. It's important to support where you get spiritually nourished.

5
GIVE 10% FOR YOUR RETIREMENT

Come grow old with me, the best is yet to be.
—Poet Robert Browning
to wife, Elizabeth

Your second expense is for your retirement.
Why do this?
If you can tell me—without breaking out in hysterical laughter—that your Social Security pension will be enough for your retirement years, then don't follow me.

According to surveys, only two percent of people above the age of 60 are financially independent. ninety eight percent of senior citizens depend on their Social Security pensions (God have mercy on them), charitable institutions, and the generosity of their relatives.

Do you want to be part of the 98 percent or the two percent?

If you want to be part of the 2% who are financially independent, set aside ten percent of your monthly income and put it in pension plans, the money market, mutual funds, and other less-risky investments. Ask other more qualified people who are professionals in this field where to build your safety net.

I've heard some preachers say Christians shouldn't save because it shows a lack of trust in God. I disagree. I believe that as stewards of His wealth, it's our responsibility to save for our future.

Give ten percent for your retirement.

ACTION PLAN

Ask around for people who can help you find a safe place for your savings to grow. For your retirement savings, the lesser the risk, the better. Always shop around before you invest.

6
GIVE 10% FOR CREATING ASSETS

Profits are better than wages.
—Jim Rohn

People complain, "Banks are the only ones that are getting rich nowadays!"

I tell them, "Stop complaining. Just do what the banks do and you'll get rich too." How? Stop borrowing money. Because when you borrow money, you get charged interest—and the banks get rich.

Do as the banks do: Lend money and charge interest.

By that, I mean create assets.

What are assets?

I love Robert Kiyosaki's definition in *Rich Dad, Poor Dad*. He said assets are anything that puts money in your pocket without you directly working for it.

If you invested in pension plans, mutual funds and stocks, these are paper assets—because through interest or dividends, they put money in your pocket without you directly working for it. In other words, you're like a bank. You're lending people money and charging interest.

If you own a candy machine, a taxi, a beauty parlor, a rental home, a multinational corporation or a fishball cart—that's an asset. These things put money in your pocket as well.

Why are assets better than direct labor? Because you only have so many hours to work. But there's no limit to the number of assets you can own.

Let me give you an example. Just to gain a financial education no school can give me, I bought a fishball cart worth P100,000 and asked someone to manage it for me. Minus all my expenses, I earn P3,500 a month without me lifting a finger. Peanuts, you say.

But that means I earn a whopping 42 percent interest per year, while a savings account in my bank gives me only one percent a year.

And what if I tell you that I'm thinking of expanding to ten carts?

Every month, set aside another ten percent to create assets—whether paper assets or business ventures that you want to experiment with.

Give ten percent for creating assets.

ACTION PLAN

Remember our discussion on "Tilling the Soil of Your Mind." Don't invest with cash first. Invest your time in study, research and training.

7

BE READY FOR SOME SEEDS TO FAIL

Success is going from failure to failure without loss of enthusiasm.
—*Winston Churchill*

Not all the seeds you planted will sprout.

Not every sales call you make will become a sale.

Not every business you start will succeed.

But people don't like that.

One time, I advised a friend, "Try starting a small business."

He answered, "I tried doing that but I failed. I guess I'm really an employee-type of a person."

"Hmm. And how many businesses did you try?"

His answer, "One."

Wow.

Since then, I've changed my advice. I now tell people, "Try to fail in nine businesses."

I'm driving home the point that you've got to fail if you want to learn.

It's a common fact that nine out of ten small business ventures don't last after five years. Well, that simply means you've got to fail nine times before you succeed!

That's better than the lotto ticket you buy: Your chances of succeeding are one in thirteen million. But how many people buy lotto tickets every day?

Let me ask you a question. Have you ever taught your baby to walk?

You position his chubby feet on the floor, and you say, "Come to Mama!"

Naturally, he falls on his face and cries like a police siren.

If you're the mother, what do you say? "Oh poor baby, you're really not meant for walking. I guess you'll be a crawler for life."

You don't do that! Even if your baby falls three hundred thousand times, you won't give up until he walks.

But why do we give up in business if we've fallen flat on our faces a few times?

Remember: If you learn from your failure, it's no longer a failure.

You've made it a successful failure.

Be ready for some seeds to fail.

ACTION PLAN

Though there are exceptions, I recommend that you don't resign from your job to start a business. Keep your day job and start something on the side. And don't invest lots of cash in a business until you've failed a couple of times!

8

SEARCH FOR YOUR MILLIONS IN THE LITTLE THINGS

Little drops of water wear down big stones.
—Russian Proverb

Let me give you a scenario.

If you save P2,000 each month (that's P66 a day) at ten percent annual interest, you'll have P146,522 at the end of five years.

Hopefully though, on your sixth year, you'd have had a few salary increases along the way. So you decide to increase your savings to P3,000 a month. By your eleventh year, you decide to save P4,500 a month. By your sixteenth year, you increase it to P6,750 per month.

In 20 years, you would have accumulated P2,428,339.

Just by saving (at the start) P66 a day.

For example, I didn't know that a pack of cigarettes now cost P30. Can you believe the waste? If you smoke two packs a day, and stopped, then invested the money instead in the same way, you'd have a million pesos in 20 years.

So when you smoke, you really burn a million pesos.

Age	Monthly Savings	Total Savings
30 years old	0 per month	P0.00
31 years old	P2,000 per month	P24,000
36 years old	P3,000 per month	P197,175
41 years old	P4,500 per month	P555,335
46 years old	P6,750 per month	P1,251,048
51 years old	0 per month	P2,428,339

Naturally, your question to me will be, "Bo, where in the world can I find something that gives ten percent interest? Banks give only one to three percent interest rates."

Believe me, it's out there. As of this writing, there are mutual funds based on a mix of government bonds and stocks that give a low return of five percent to a high return of 15 percent per year.

Again, you'll have to ask people better qualified than I am to answer these questions.

In the meantime, here's a few saving tips from Hans Jakobi in his book *How to be Rich & Happy on Your Income*.

- Bring a home-cooked lunch and snacks to work.
- Let your kids bring home-cooked lunch to school.
- Eliminate frozen food from your shopping and freeze your own.
- Shop no more than once a week.
- Stay away from shops when you're depressed.
- Try generic brands.
- Shop when it's genuine sale items.
- Plan your gift spending; better, make your own gifts.
- Stop gambling. Lotto tickets accumulate!
- Make your own entertainment by taking picnics and going for walks.

Search for your millions in the little things.

ACTION PLAN
I bet you can discover better ways of saving. Think!

9

SET YOUR MIND ON HOW MUCH YOU WANT TO EARN

*Then the LORD your God will make you most prosperous
in all the work of your hands…*
—Deuteronomy 30:9

Here's something that all parents are familiar with.

When my son was a baby, he'd wake up in the middle of the night and cry like he was being roasted on an open fire. "Waaaaaaaaaaaaaah!" So I'd jump out of bed and think he must have a tummy ache. I'd lift his shirt, expose that soft belly that's as round as a ball, and swab on three ointments I bought from three different countries: China, Thailand and Indonesia. His response was firm. "Waaaaaaaaaaaaaah!"

Nope, it wasn't the tummy. Oh, it must be his diapers, I'd groan. Why didn't I think of that? So I'd raise his chubby legs, strip the old diaper and strap a fresh one on in 9.7 seconds, plus ten minutes. The result? "Waaaaaaaaaaaaaah!"

I'd go to the act of last resort. I'd pick him up for a song-and-dance routine. "Rocka-a-by-baby-on-a-treetop…" (Who ever wrote that song is sick. Who in his right mind would put a baby on top of a tree?) And after 30 minutes of the waltz, cha-cha, boogie, and disco and non-stop crying, I'd give up.

Totally exasperated, I'd kneel in front of him and beg for mercy, "PLEASE, TELL ME WHAT YOU WANT! JUST TALK! I'LL GIVE IT TO YOU!"

His answer?

"Waaaaaaaaaaaaaah!"

I compare my son to many people today.

Do you know why many people fail to get what they want?

Because they don't know what they want.

And the whole universe is kneeling in front of them, asking, begging, pleading, "What do you want? I'll give it to you! Just tell me what you want!"

But they don't. They just cry, "Waaaaaaaaaaaaaah!"

For example, when I ask people what they want in life, they answer, "I want to be happy."

Gosh. "Can you be more general than that?"

Dreams are powerless unless they are specific.

So I try again. "What does happiness mean to you?"

So they rattle off things like, "A well-paying job."

When I press them and ask, "How well-paying is well-paying? How much do you want to earn?" they start to laugh and change the subject.

Listen. If you don't have a specific figure, this whole goals thing won't work.

It's got to be specific!

One day, I came before God and calculated how much I needed for my family's needs and how much I wanted to give to Him. I then got a piece of paper and wrote down how much I wanted to earn 12   months later.

I made the figure big but not unreasonably so.

And every morning, I'd look at that figure, and pray for it.

Twelve months after, I was earning exactly the amount I scribbled on that piece of paper. This thing really works!

I noticed that as I prayed for my financial goals each day, I felt my mind open up to possibilities. And I felt the whole universe open up to me! It was supplying all that I needed to reach my goals.

Set your mind on how much you want to earn.

ACTION PLAN

Go to a quiet place. Get a piece of paper. How much do you want to earn by this month next year? Write a figure that will cover your needs and the amount you want to give to the Lord's work. Stick that piece of paper in a place that you can see each morning. Pray for it every day. And see what happens.

10
TALK ABOUT YOUR FINANCES AS A COUPLE

*If you want your spouse to listen and pay strict attention to
every word you say, talk in your sleep.*
—*Anonymous*

This was the night of all nights.

In the living room of her parents' house, I knelt on my
right knee, held her hand, and asked my one and only true
love, "Will you marry me?"

After much equivocating, the girl of my dreams
answered, "Yes." (Equivocating meant she first rolled on
the floor for half an hour, almost dying of laughter.)

On that day, we also agreed not only to prepare for our
wedding but for our marriage. So instead of just talking
about the color motif, the menu of the reception and how
low the neckline of her gown should be (until her lower
lip), we also read together Christian marriage books.

So even before we got married, we already talked about
our finances.

We talked about simplicity, budgeting, savings,
investments, expenditures and the kind of shopping I
allow (window).

And when we got married, we continued to have regular discussions on our finances.

Why do we do this?

Because surveys say that fighting about money is the number one reason for divorce. Can you believe that? More couples separate because of financial disagreements rather than marital infidelity and horrible mothers-in-law.

Couples need to agree how to run their finances if they want their marriage to last.

Talk about your finances as a couple.

ACTION PLAN

Schedule at least once a month for you and your spouse to sit down and discuss topics contained in this book.

11
YOU RUN YOUR OWN COMPANY AND YOU'RE THE PRODUCT

*When you start doing what you really love to do,
you'll never work another day in your life.*
—Brian Tracy

One day, a friend of mine realized that the company he was working for was financially going down the toilet. In six months, he knew it would belly-flop.

I met him in a mall eating his pizza, as though he had no problems in the world.

When he spoke up, I realized why.

He said, "Bo, my customers have been after me for years. They told me that should I want to jump ship, to please consider them. I've got a stack of their calling cards in my drawer waiting to be called. Besides, if they won't hire me, I know you would, right?" He continued to eat his pizza.

The guy was right. I'd hire him on the spot. I wouldn't even let him finish his pizza.

Why? Because my friend is one of the most effective administrators I've ever met in my life. In a world of half-jobs and sloppy tasks, he delivers. You tell him to take care of a project and you can forget about that project. It's as good as done.

No wonder companies are after him.

Haven't you noticed?

No matter what the economic mood is in the world, there'll be people who'll be making it big? And even in the bleakest of recessions, there'll still be people who'll be raking it in and prospering?

I believe that how much you earn doesn't depend on the company that you work for. (Temporarily, it might, but never in the long-term.) Nor does it depend on the economic cycle of the world.

I believe how much you earn depends on one person: You.

I don't care if you're an employee working for a huge company. The truth of the matter is, you really work for yourself.

You run your own service company, and the product of that company is you.

So polish that product.

Improve it daily.

Make it the best product customers will die for.

You run your company and you're the product.

ACTION PLAN

Do a quality check of your Product. Seek to have raving fans.

12
LET YOUR WORK BE YOUR WORSHIP

If a man is called to be a streetsweeper, he should sweep
even as Michaelangelo painted, or Beethoven composed music,
or Shakespeare wrote poetry. He should sweep streets so well
that all the host of heaven and earth will pause to say,
"Here lived a streetsweeper who did his job well."
—Martin Luther King Jr.

Your job should worship God.

Because you're not employed by your boss or company, but by God Himself.

The fat guy with the bad breath behind the desk in front of you isn't your boss.

The Almighty is your real Boss.

St. Paul says, "Whatever you do, work at it with all your heart, as working for the Lord, not for men... It is the Lord Christ you are serving."[10]

So when you give sloppy work, you give sloppy worship to God.

I remember Joseph in the Old Testament.

Wherever he was working—whether as a slave in Potiphar's house, a jailbird in an Egyptian prison or as Vice-Pharaoh, he was always Star Employee of the year.

No, he didn't do these for the awards.

He just did a fine job everywhere he went because he was faithful to God.

This is what I learned: If you work for God, you bloom wherever you're planted.

So respect and honor that fat guy with the bad breath behind the desk in front of you. He doesn't look it, but he's God's representative.

Again, St. Paul says, "Slaves, obey your earthly masters with respect and fear, and with sincerity of heart, just as you would obey Christ. Serve wholeheartedly, as if you were serving the Lord, not men…"[11]

Let your work be worship.

ACTION PLAN

Will you be embarrassed when you present your work to the Lord as your worship? Or will you be proudly offering your work to Him? What can you do to make your work more pleasing to God? List down the ways.

13
LET YOUR PROFESSION BE YOUR PULPIT

*It is no use walking anywhere to preach unless
our walking is our preaching.*
—St. Francis of Assisi

I'm not the only preacher here.

I believe you preach as well. The difference is that if my audience doesn't like what I say, they stand and leave the room.

You, however, have a captive audience in your workplace listening to you eight hours a day, five days a week. If your audience doesn't like what you preach, they're stuck with you, and they'll have to listen to your preaching whether they like it or not.

But here's the situation: You and I can preach two Gospels.

You can either preach the Gospel of Christ.

Or you can preach the Gospel of Satan.

If you live a life that follows his teachings of materialism, selfishness and pride—then you create hell in your office and train them for the real hell in the future.

If you live a life of love, forgiveness and humility, then you preach the Gospel of Heaven—and bring your officemates closer to that place.

The choice is yours.

Let your profession be your pulpit.

ACTION PLAN

Do your officemates become better persons because of knowing you and being with you? Find out how you can bless them and bring them closer to God.

14
LOVE YOUR CUSTOMERS

*You can have everything in life that you want
if you'll just help enough other people to get what they want.*
—Zig Ziglar

I have friends who got their jobs not for their skills but for their personal integrity.

They were basically honest people because they loved God—and companies wanted them for their Purchasing Department—a fertile place for corruption.

I know customers love honesty as well.

Businesses that are known for their integrity will win customer loyalty, and thus, a rosier bottom line.

Companies talk a lot about service these days. "We put the customer first" is the ad line of many brands in this age. But don't you notice? They've just changed the words. They've reworded a biblical principle.

So whenever I lecture at companies about "customers first" programs, I just tell employees to love their customers, period.

Let them feel they're special to you.

Let them tell you what they want—and exceed those wants. Wow them.

Let them know that they're your friends—not just buyers of your product.

Love your customers.

ACTION PLAN

Who are your customers? If you're working in a huge company, you may not even see your end customer. But your officemates who need your output are your customers. Love them. Care for them. Serve them.

15

GIVE YOUR WIDOW'S MITE

Don't give until it hurts.
Give until it feels good.
—James Kidd

I believe in proportional giving.

If God has blessed me more, I don't see why I'm going to give only ten percent. I should give 20 percent or 30 percent or more.

Before you throw this seditious book away, let me explain.

If my neighbor earns P5,000 a month, his ten percent is 500 bucks.

If I earn P50,000 a month, my ten percent is P5,000.

You might say, "That's fair enough."

I don't think so. You see, the percentage isn't as important as what's left behind after we give. My neighbor will have P4,500 left while I still have P45,000 left.

Proportional giving is the "widow's mite" principle in the Bible. In the story, Jesus wasn't impressed with the rich men who dropped heavy bags of gold to the temple treasury. He was impressed with the widow who clunked in two copper coins because she had nothing left, but those rich guys had heaps of gold in their banks.[12]

When you give to God, how much is left behind?

Remember: There's joy in giving. If you give more, you receive more of His joy—and blessing.

Give your widow's mite.

ACTION PLAN
As you simplify your life, try to give a bigger offering each year than the previous year.

EPILOGUE

NEVER FORGET THE LESSONS OF THE DESERT

God doesn't mind you having money,
but He minds money having you.
—T.D. Jakes

At the beginning of this book, I told you how at the age of 13, I wanted to live in total simplicity for God. I told you how I threw my clothes away, didn't comb my hair and stopped putting deodorant.

You could just imagine the dramatic impact I had on a crowd. My friends told me I had superpowers. I was like one of those televangelists: All I had to do was raise my hand and a whole crowd of people would fall.

But I didn't mention something at the start of this book.

Twenty years ago, if you had any kind of savings, I'd tell you that you lacked faith.

Twenty years ago, if you invested in insurance, pension funds and mutual funds, I'd say you were spiritually immature.

And 20 years ago, if you talked about business and money, I'd command you to repent and fix your eyes on things above.

It's amazing how 20 years later, I'm writing a book telling people that as good Christian stewards, we should save, invest, and think about money.

By the way, did I say I now use deodorant?

But in all these wild changes in my life, one thing has not changed: I still live the simple life.

And my definition remains the same: Simplicity means living from the core of my being.[13] And what is my core?

God.

That has not changed.

And I've discovered the key to always having Simple Abundance: While living in the Promised Land, never forget the lessons of the desert.

Never forget that to receive blessings is not the goal.

The goal is to give the blessings away.

Have fun giving them away.

Bo

P.S. If you wish to contact me, write to **bomail@shepherdsvoice.com.ph.** I'd love to hear from you. And if you want to receive a free e-mail newsletter from me every week, send write to **soulfood@shepherdsvoice.com.ph.** See you!

FOOTNOTES

[1] Please know that the Promised Land's primary meaning in the Bible is spiritual salvation, heaven, and total well-being—not financial success. But because this book is about finances, I'm focusing on a secondary or peripheral meaning of the Promised Land—what I call Simple Abundance in our finances and lifestyle.

[2] Luke 11:3

[3] Philippians 4:12-13

[4] Luke 14:12-14

[5] Even our dog and cat are poor.

[6] I changed her name to protect her privacy.

[7] It will be very easy to make you happy.

[8] John 12:3-6

[9] See 1 Corinthians 16:2

[10] Colossians 3:23-24

[11] Ephesians 6:5-7

[12] Luke 21:1-4

[13] Janet Luhrs, *The Simple Living Guide*

<u>COMING SOON!</u>

THE LAST INSTALLMENT OF BO'S SIMPLIFY TRILOGY:

Book I: Simplify and Live the Good Life
Book 2: Simplify and Create Abundance
Book 3: SIMPLIFY AND...

WATCH FOR IT AT THE BOOKSTORE NEAREST YOU NEXT YEAR!

SUBSCRIBE TO KERYGMA!
The #1 Inspirational Magazine in the Country

Bo Sanchez is the main writer of KERYGMA, the #1 inspirational magazine in the country. Get a whole year subscription of 12 exciting issues for only P420 (plus P60 for provincial subscribers). Feed your soul with God's Word at this affordable price!

Call us at (02) 411-7874 to 77, or e-mail us at **sale@shepherdsvoice.com.ph**, or write to Shepherd's Voice, #60 Chicago St., Cubao, Quezon City 1109. Check out our website at **www.shepherdsvoice.com.ph**.

Subscribe now! You'll be blessed 12 times a year!

ATTEND THE KERYGMA FEAST!

Each month, Bo Sanchez preaches at the KERYGMA Feast. Join us for Holy Mass, inspiring worship, prayers for healing, and the dynamic Preaching of God's Word.

- In Quezon City, it's held at Bulwagang Heneral Arturo Enrile, Camp Aguinaldo, Quezon City, every 1st Sunday of the month, 7:30 a.m. or 10:00 a.m. or 3:00 p.m.
- In Cebu City, it's held at Grand Convention Center, Archbishop Reyes Avenue, every 1st Monday of the month, 7:00 p.m.
- In Iloilo, it's held at CAP Development Center, Gen. Luna St., every 1st Wednesday of the month, 6:00 p.m.

For more information, call us at (02) 411-7874 to 77.

BE PART OF GIVING GOD'S LOVE TO OTHERS!

Be one of Bo Sanchez' TV Partners and help spread God's love through TV!

TV programs are expensive, but they reach millions of people with the message of hope and love and healing. Help us keep our power-packed TV shows on air by praying for us and giving a monthly pledge. We're looking for 1000 people who will give P1000 a month—or any amount really—so that we can continue broadcasting His Word to more people.

Call us at (02) 411-7874 to 77, or e-mail us at sale@shepherdsvoice.com.ph or write to Shepherd's Voice, #60 Chicago St., Cubao, Quezon City 1109. Check out our website at **www.shepherdsvoice.com.ph**.

ABOUT THE AUTHOR

 Bo Sanchez is main writer and publisher of *Kerygma,* which is read by more people than any other inspirational magazine in the country. He is also writer of many best-selling books, including *You Have the Power to Create Love*, *Simplify and Live the Good Life*, and *Thank God He's Boss*. He is the founder of many organizations, two of them being ANAWIM, a dynamic ministry for the poor, and the LIGHT OF JESUS Community. He began preaching at the age of 13 and hasn't stopped ever since. He lives with his wife Marowe and sons Benedict Thomas and Francis John in Manila, Philippines.

You may write to him at **bomail@shepherdsvoice.com.ph.**